Praise for

Postcards

"An amazing read that offers valuable life lessons and a deeper understanding of the human experience. . . . [Jo's] ability to craft a narrative that draws the reader in and keeps them captivated is a testament to her skill as a writer. . . . a must-read for anyone looking for a thought-provoking and emotionally resonant literary experience."

—DOREEN CHOMBU for Readers' Favorite

"Immerse yourself in a captivating collection of observational poetry and slice-of-life stories with *Postcards* . . . one of those rare collections that will appeal to a broad spectrum of readers from pretty much any background. I recommend you not miss out on this one!"

—PIKASHO DEKA for Readers' Favorite

"Poet and author Jo Taylor has a rare gift. . . . Equally adept at free verse, rhyming, and metered poetic forms, as well as the short story, Taylor moves seamlessly from one to the next in adroit and often surprising ways. . . . For a truly engaging and artfully diversified reading experience, *Postcards* is a sure winner."

—GOLDER HAZELTON for Readers' Favorite

"[Jo's] needle-art reflections mirror her thoughts on life, her perspective of all that matters, and thoughtful inspirational interpretation of everything that was, is, and perhaps will be. . . . a literary collage of thoughts and memories that will have readers thinking more deeply about their own postcard moments. . . . . a book that needs to be savored over time."

—EMILY-JANE HILLS ORFORD for Readers' Favorite

"Read along and be enthralled . . . *Postcards* has a melodic ring as [Jo] lets us into her world. . . . Appreciating the beautiful things around us we take for granted is one theme that runs through the entire anthology . . . which showcases a lovely harmony between poetry and prose."

—ESSIEN ASIAN for Readers' Favorite

Postcards

POSTCARDS

Collected Poems

and

Short Stories

❧

Jo Taylor

Road Clothes PRESS

Published 2024
Printed in the United States of America
Hardcover ISBN: 978-1-962504-01-0
Paperback ISBN: 978-1-962504-02-7
E-ISBN: 978-1-962504-03-4
Library of Congress Control Number: 2024910754

Road Clothes Press
Daphne, AL 36526
Roadclothespress.com

Book design by Stacey Aaronson

The poems and short stories included in this volume are
either reflections on my own experience or are fictitious.
In certain cases, names and identifying characteristics
have been changed to protect the privacy of specific
individuals.

*To my husband, Kevin, who supported my decision to
leave work and write because it made me happy.
I love you.*

*To my son, Jake, who is the embodiment of the sentiment
that a child is your heart walking around outside you
I love you.*

*To my sweet dog, Abby, who sat by my side and missed
many pets as my hands were busy on the keys.
I loved you.*

Contents

Poems

Faith, or Lack Thereof

❧

Love, or Something Like It

❧

Death and Medicine

❧

Life, the Past, and History

Postcards . . . 45

Short Stories

Poems

Faith, or
Lack
Thereof

Sister Mary

She sat in the front pew like a first-chair violin.
Ready, waiting, ever waiting
for a sign from the Conductor.
The beads in her hands passed through fingers
that couldn't have known hard work.
They were so soft and cool
against my cheek when I would fret,
and Sister Mary
calmly reassured.

There had to be something wrong
with a woman who didn't want men
to think her pretty, or babies to rush to her
skirts with laughter or tears.
I had the urge to call her
Sister Mary Elephant
and I was scared it would fly out of my mouth one day
when I wasn't
fully in control.

The other nuns sat scattered in the pews
like burly seeds resting on top of the ground
before the wind covers them with dirt.

It would be a good place for them.
In the ground,
covered with dirt.

They made me feel like I was in
the way, a penance they must attend to
before being given their rightful place
outside under the oak tree
where bugs crawled and rows of marble
stapled the grass.
No thanks, I'd rather go to Africa to hear the
silence of the Serengeti
and risk my soul for being lusted after.

Someday, when my skin cleared
and my chest grew.

And on a day when I was twenty-six,
I sat alone in a booth at a coffee shop
fretting over the last worthless man to leave me
just hours before
and the waitress talked in a low, sweet, heavenly voice
of loading rocks into a wheelbarrow in Africa
to make a road
by hand
and I didn't see anything wrong with her.

Communion

Bright burst of song erupted in the loft.
A cannon 'round my soul to lift it up.
I walked the aisle to the saving cup.
Fine decrescendo brought the music soft.

To counterpoint of sin and grace I went.
No dissonance of pitch to make me pause.
The gift of blood and body, heaven sent,
was written on the clef of human flaws.

A plainsong filled the air as I received
the harmony of heaven's saving grace.
Sweet, perfect intonation filled the space.
My sorrows washed away, my sins relieved.
No proof redemption earned, but I believed.

Unending Thread

Unending thread between your heart and mine,
awaits the tug of distance to reveal
a purpose borne of using the divine
to lose our forms yet strengthen soul's appeal

that we not tarry in the ether mist
behind a tattered veil for feigned delight.
Sweet nymphs and stirred emotion, lightly kissed,
are not the true love promised by the night.

The thread pulls back; we reel through space and time
believing all we see is here and now.
Illumination bares the truth in rhyme,
existence rests its head on lover's brow.

Returning from the dream to find you there,
a halo brume encircling your hair.

Again, I want to sleep and travel far,
beyond the earthly bound'ries of my form,
and meet you near the heavens' blazing star.
The kindly light feels safe and free and warm.

We circle 'round the azure-shrouded world.

The thread has bound us surely down the nave.
Remains of day and night before unfurled
and carried on a crimson, golden wave.

Forever, we will journey through this life.
No fear of crossing to the farther plane.
Between the two, the best room truly rife
with charity and love in His domain.

No matter if we wake or if we sleep,
Love's bond, a truer marriage couldn't keep.

2010 Published in *Tapestry: Poetic Threads of Life.*
Palm Springs, CA: Omega Publications, pp. 194.

Four

I saw four planets in the
early morning January sky.
The closest and the biggest
competing for my attention and the
coordinates of my telescope.
By four a.m., the sky hadn't changed.
The sun didn't rise below
Venus, Mars, Jupiter, Saturn,
the four horses of the apocalypse
or just my own miracle.
The news didn't say anything about
my discovery,
but night fell at four in the afternoon
and I knew we stopped too.

Mend the Veil

It is not my grief.

I was not a close friend or family,
but I knew you.
Knew enough to see
the charm and grace that only heaven
bestows upon His angels here on earth.

You wrote three days before your death:
"I don't want to leave with a
'why didn't I?'"

Prophetic
maybe, but that was just the way you were.
Living, smiling, putting the rest of us to shame with the
petty complaints you had no time for.
We didn't know you had
no time.

Tangled in the web of accident, we lost you,
and we lose
until they come out the other side of grief,
the friends who played a part,
cast in a play they had no knowledge of
until now.

It was an accident.
It ended your life and changes theirs forever.
What do the rest of us say, or do, to bring them
whole to the other side of grief?

We love them as much as we love you.

Our calling is to save lives, and to take one
shears every fiber of the fabric weaving
us together.

Give us new thread, let us mend the
torn veil between life and death, so they are
not compelled to follow you,
not yet.

It is not my grief.

Life's Tenuous Thread

Stitch together
a plan that has the weight
of warp and weft,
of tactile probability in the
face of absolute uncertainty.

Mend the tears and rifts
of life's tenuous thread
that decays by
no uncertain terms
from random chaos,
something neither you nor I can
prevent or disinherit from our lives.

Deal with it.

Put the big girl panties on and
lead us all
through the coming crumble of
order into a bleak and tired shell
that pretends to be the future
and out again into the palest hue of hope,
the softest ray of light
from far away and long ago.

Discover the repaired and fortified
new,
the shell,
the silk with softest
hand and hold it against
the cheek of humanity lest we
forget that we were born to create and
not destroy.

Jesus Was an INFJ

Lauren and Paula and I all sit
hunched over our coffee
on the patio
that looked from inside like it
should be warm
but it's not

We don't go back in

Too easy to give up and not
fight for quality time
even if it is freezing and
my back cramps
and I can't feel
the back of my hands while
the palms get burned by the
white mug

We are INFJ's
the type that is only two percent of the population
and yet we find each other
and stick together
impervious to outside scrutiny

INFJ's are the counselors
We listen, absorb
feelings from others
even if it's toxic and burns
from the inside out

"Jesus was an INFJ," Paula says

We nod our heads as if that
explains so much

Wonderful, Counselor,
the Mighty God, the Everlasting Father,
The Prince of Peace

Only one Myers Briggs Type
is mentioned in Handel's Messiah

It's a sign
that we are right
and the rest of the world is wrong

We choose our few, this tiny circle
and expend energy in our meetings
never taking from others
always giving

But it's easier with this crowd

The future is more real than the present
big picture more clear than up close
abstract better than concrete and
details be damned

We want to be alone like Garbo, but
must be sure everyone else is good first

I can see Jesus plan his sermons,
call up a miracle,
know how life will end and does not leave
a credit open at the feed store

His inner life charged with rich and vivid images
of the way he wanted the world to be
hurt by what he saw in reality, but
didn't tell anyone
only his closest friends,
withdrew from some and left
them confused and upset
and maybe abandoned

hurt enough to betray.

Love, or
Something
Like It

Baseball Glove

Fingers starched.
Leather the color of raw honeycomb.

You smelled of summer and fresh cut grass and the
musty barn
at the end of O'Donovan Road.

I worked you until you felt like a hand without bones,
thrilled at your yaw open and closed.

Your ties between my teeth
anchored me in place on the dusty, brown grass field.

You never let me down.

Pop couldn't be bothered to show for a game but
bragged about what a great kid he had.

Fingers soft.
Leather the color of grass-covered hills in July.

You followed me to college, content to stay in the dorm
while I studied, and partied, and fell in love.

When my son was born,
I dreamed of playing catch with him.

But he loved solitary pursuits like archery and running.

So I went to matches and meets, put you away in a box
with my college things,
and my letterman jacket, and the 4H medals for my
champion pigs.

Pop didn't see those things either.

Fingers slack.
Leather the color of ten-second tea.

I carried his running shorts and arrow tips to the car.
He appeared with you on his hand and set you in the
box with his college things.
He said you were like holding my hand.

You stayed in the dorm while he studied and partied
and fell in love.

Fingers worn.
Leather the color of palm tree bark.
He brought you, grey with age, to say goodbye.
He promised to keep you safe,
to pass you on to his little boy.

"You never let me down."

Honorable

I bring paper to your office.
The perfect excuse to say hello
and look for a faint color
in your face that says you are
self-conscious when I stop
to talk to you about the weather
or the color blue you wore today.

In the halls, we slow and talk,
each time a little closer
than the last, until the space is
too confined and we push apart
like magnets set wrong end to end.

You call me as I reach for the phone
to call you about some silly favor
or to ask a question I've known
the answer to for years.

Tomorrow, I'll ask you if you'd like to meet for coffee.

Today I hope to see you just once
so I can add that moment to
the collection of memories I've made

of the places we begin
and add it to my dreams
of the places we could go.

Elusive Point

I stood on the road that led to you,
black asphalt shimmering in the
August heat,
oppressive air in a watery
ribbon through the middle of my vision.
No curves to garner interest,
no dips to thrill me,
only the telescoping future,
the artist's rendering of perspective,
a pinpoint of oblivion on the horizon.
The edges of the road converged in the distance,
past my influence and reach.

I stood on the road that led to you
on a Tuesday four years later, but the
October sky
blended with the pale remnant,
intense heat and persistent sunlight had stolen the color,
leaving it like the back of a mirror,
dull gray and without the movement of
atoms rising quickly from the surface.

I stand on the road that leads to youth,
December wind
at my back,

fingering memories like the pearls of my necklace.
The road doesn't lead to you anymore.

Your presence is reflected in the blunted gray road,
the specter of you
always somewhere in the elusive point
where the road disappears into the limit and the mind
imagines the infinite.

Distant Cousin

Loneliness is here.

She's not a friend, but I entertain her now and then.
I'm duty bound to be a gracious hostess
for this distant cousin of Joy.

Dull, lifeless conversations about this group and that,
of which I have no part,
drive me to the cold glass of the winter window.

To escape her, I place my cheek against the pane and
feel the sharp, harsh
coldness of the glass, relieved to feel something besides
loneliness's empty ache.

In an effort to make her go,
I act silly and call out the window to birds,
wishing they would come inside and be my friends.

She sits and sips her tea.
I return to my place beside her.
Silently, we nibble on tasteless biscuits,
and I check my watch again and again,
wondering when it will be time for

Loneliness to leave.

Paper and Time

I hardly ever check the mail
expecting to see your smallish hand
addressed to me—it makes me pale
and from the script I sense demand

of time and thought I'd rather spend
on someone else, not you, no more.
I turn the letter over and pretend
for now that I won't open a door,

a tiny flap, to let you creep
into my life again, with sorrow
in your actor's voice, so deep
and luscious that night becomes 'morrow

without so much as a breath
between us, only paper and time.
Once it was supposed to be "until death,"
but now is merely written in the line.

Handsome Face

A handsome face
I look and look again,
eyes wandering to other, less captivating views
lest I be found out
then back again once more before he rushes
out of sight into the belly of the city.

With sidelong glance I search
in the minutia of eye and brow,
lip and cheek,
for the answer to why my eyes
are drawn to his and what it is I hope to
know about him.

Symmetry is beauty
found in flower, nautilus, and human face.
Symmetry of form and ratio,
a mathematical explanation for
the beauty I see peeking out
from under his black umbrella.

Beauty is in the familiar and the divine,
So, too, we find in faces the match to self or God.
We imprint qualities of likeness,
so alike as to understand us,

or divinity such that they are worthy of adoration
simply by how he looks

and so, I always search in crowds for
a handsome face.

It Will Matter

I may never see you again.
It will matter, but it will not make a difference.

Surely, immediately, you effected a
refinement of my thought,
inscribed in humble degree
upon an unsuspecting canvas;
outlined until now with heart and soul,
but not with understanding.

Swiftly, you drew in the shades of gray
I failed to see in others.

Too cryptically, I spoke of lessons to be
learned, and my wavering surety of your role.
Too soon, I felt the weight of expectation,
and doubt that men and women could be
friends and nothing more.

Your existence is a comfort
I can neither define nor embrace.

That I can stand outside myself and
see what is supposed to be, what is destined,

is an odd and painful thing; when all I
ever expected was to be able to love you
for who you were, not for who I was.

Lined Yellow Paper

I took the lovely, lined, yellow paper
turned it sideways
wrote in fluid script
so I could see
words march boldly on the page
their rank and rhythm
blue line bound
pinned through letters
like stakes hold trees in perfect place
steadfast and true.

Words no longer held up
like socks or dresses hung to dry
clipped here and there to flutter
in the warm August breeze

Blue lines pushed them forward like
waves to the beach,
onward to meaning or truth
or not.

Your careless words left lying
on the clean-swept floor,
written sideways on legal yellow,

meant that you weren't pinned
in place anymore, free from
boundaries, blue line waves
pushed to a different shore

and carried you with them.

Death

and

Medicine

On Her Way to Zero

Below her
sounds of the city
tumble along
skyscraper canyon walls

Birds
like black freckles
on the face of a distant dome
too far away to see wings flap
or hear the caws

With an eagle eye
she notes the time on the clock
two stories down

A note tucked in the bodice
of her yellow-flowered summer dress

His careless words
left lying on the clean-swept floor

Her descent is as calm as
stepping off her mother's porch

No frantic hands

no fierce grabs at air that
will not save her

on her way to zero

Published in San Luis Obispo, CA Telegram Tribune,
Sunday, April 4, 2010
Published in Tapestry Poetic Threads of Life by
Omega Publications, 2010

Three Souls

Jake rolls through the ER doors at
seven-fourteen p.m. and
his soul stands outside, watches,
waits for us to catch on that
he's not in there anymore.
No heartbeat, no breathing,
eyes fixed on the ceiling,
twenty-year-old body like a
broken doll on the gurney.

Sally's chest moves up and down,
breath sounds loud enough
to hear down the hall or miles away.
No one sits beside her bed, fingers entwined
to keep her from leaving,
cold metal rails the only border between there and here,
and she slips there when no one is watching.

Tom totters in at half past three,
awakened from fretful sleep
by quiet next to him.
He turned the light to find her lined face pale,
eyes open and staring at the ceiling.

He sat in the front seat,
carried along in confused silence,
wondering if he locked the door
after the men in black pants that smelled of smoke.

There are not enough of us to compress and
shock and poke and breathe and comfort,
so the last gets dropped and Tom sits alone
in a room full of people,
clutching a wadded-up tissue,
staring at her soul looking out of
stationary eyes that don't water or blink.

Choice of Truth

Does he want the truth
when he asks me if
he's going to die?
Or does he seek a platitude
that sucks the danger back inside
and does not let it dance around for all to see?

We do not say such things aloud.
As if, in word, we make them true.
But they are true whether
we give verbal life to them,
Or not.

Death and taxes, so they say—the only truth
in every life.

No tax today, but death will come.
I nod my head, eyes locked on his
and a smile plays around his lips.
"Good girl," he whispers
and pats the hand that seeks to dam the flow of blood.
Approval for my choice of truth
plain in the
relief of his brow,

the last sigh of breath,
the small stroke of his thumb across the back of my
hand.

Life,
the Past,
and
History

Postcards

I once was sweet on a Saturday in May 1974, but not
too many times since then.

Naïve disappeared along with my favorite pink cable
sweater
and the cousin who came to dinner.

Thoughtful I can muster, but it comes out like
worry and flutters around my feet.

Dramatic still serves me well when I tell a story or
light up the room with a laugh that echoes
over every sweet, naïve, thoughtful thing I've ever
said and pins them to the wall like postcards
of places I once was
and would like to go to
again.

Published online, After the Pause: Summer 2015;
June 1, 2015, page 49.

Down a Road

Traffic dawdled along a highway on a
dog day afternoon in August.

Engines groaned and crawled from
inch to inch.
Browned grass on either side
hid crickets trying to raise the dead.

Overheated air
rose shimmer-like,
way down the road,
at the ridge where heaven met the
baleful stretch of asphalt laid to hell.

Buster lolled his head out the window and sighed,
ignored birds on the fence
chirping like a choir of second graders,

as we moved painfully
away from all we knew
and looked ahead,
down a road where things
moved at a slower pace and we might

learn to look around and see what's here
between this stretch
and the next,
where a dog and his girl
dawdled along a highway in the
traffic of an August afternoon.

Making Change

Worry stands small, young, and handsome,
gentle fingers roll a greenback up and flat again.

Innocence steps up to my window,
pushes a portrait of Ben across the counter at me.

"Ones. All ones please."

Patience watches me count them out,
taps his gentle fingers until I reach one hundred.

Determination smiles, tips his head,
squares his shoulders as he walks out the door.

Compassion stops near the old man lying under the tree
outside,
and bends down quietly to place the stack
in the sleeping man's jacket pocket.

Humility sees a different way of making change.

Disappointment

From the picture, you stare at me and
when I look into your eyes
I see a gaze I've only seen once before
On the day you lost respect for who I was or
who I could ever be.

Three Things That
Happened in March

Judy Foster-Brothers broke her tailbone
sliding down her kids' playground set
with all the force of
a middle-aged American woman.

The kindergarten class at
Baum School sat in a Huey
that flew two hundred missions
in Vietnam.

Claire Foster left a piece of paper
on the railroad tracks where
the firemen would find it
when the train stopped.

Published online, Right Hand Pointing: March 15, 2015

Bruises

He comes home and shows me
his right arm, medial,
where the thrown bat hit him
and promises a bruise.
Can't see it, like you can't
see cheating when he comes
home with kisses and a
late harvest cabernet.
But it's there by morning,
dark and angry, painful,
like coarse revelations
over coffee and toast.

We Will Not Be Friends

New occupants of the house next door move
in stealth at night
while we are up when
light first tints the edge of things.

Their dress is conservative, khaki, light blue
with hints of button up
and leather shoes.

I can tell their culture is different
from ours.
No better, or worse
just different.

But not the kind of difference that
can be moved aside except with
thousands of hellos and goodbyes,

or by awkward invitations to join
each other for dinners that never
bridge the magnitude of how important

a neighbor is, especially one that comes
and goes so close to where we feel
apart from the outside world, or hope

that we have one place left where
no one knows how sensitive we are
to the rejection of being left.

No, we will not be friends.

Philosophy

She wears strength.
Seekers flock to her
and her kind will rule the world,
not because she is a
warrior princess
but because her strength
is built on the
scars accreted from daily
shear of barb and
ignoble burden of the earth,
invisible producer of
life and love.
She wears strength as a beacon
to others, not a badge
to garner attention.

I sit at her feet and
hear that life is fair
and you survive battles
unseen with scars inside
because you do not let them
end you.

Her earth mother
shape calls the
seekers of knowledge
and a new wisdom
comes.

Red Silk

Red silk in allegorical place on center stage;
the dancer walks toward the hanging fabric,
wraps a hand in each draping piece,
pulls herself off the floor,
into three-dimensional ballet.

Red silk, two lines ascend above my view.
The dancer portrays a woman
wrapped in desire, fighting against the
pull of lust, clasping at passion, intimacy, commitment
that hover in the essence of love
like silk in hand.

Clothed in silk
the dancer breathes life
into the story she tells.
The gleam, the ease, the poise
of fable or truth,
in terms of bodies in motion
around thoughts in still.

Red silk in soundless twisting turn
reveals the dancer for who she is,
and for who we all are.

Radiator

I burned my butt on the radiator.

I was tiptoeing to look out the window,
trying to peek out at the street where boys
rode bikes and a man on the corner
sold pretty yellow tulips.

Instead, I got a sore behind and a glimpse
of Mama at the bedroom door when she came to see
what caused my cry.

Daddy says it was a white turban hat
when I ask why Mama wore a
bandage on her head.

"Anyway, you can't remember that."

I told him the floor creaked to the left of the white
cast iron and sunshine streamed in the window
making diamonds on the floor.

My two-year-old finger pointed
to Mama and then to the bare wood and
she laughed and called them angels.

He sits back in his chair and studies me,
like he doesn't know where I've come from and
what I've seen along the way.

Author of Scorn

The belief that anything
leads to freedom
of the heart,
or mind,
or broken body left to climb its
way up from the depths of oblivion
is only that, a belief.

Water blurs my vision as I walk,
making the figures before me hazy and oblique,
until the drops race down my cheeks and suddenly,
I see

all the faces who won't look me in the eye.
The author of their scorn the time that
wears us all like the wind wears rock.

They have not the feelings of age.
They still have energy and passion.
They have not yet seen the cycle of years,
season by season,
that I have seen.

No barrier exists between the young and the old,
but the young hold the old at arm's length, afraid
that what they see will be what they become.

I believe.
I believe that youth is wasted on the young.
They have no recognition of blessing,
their firm bodies and lithe movements.
I would give my heart to have appreciated what I once
was
then.

Give me back the way I was, if only for a moment.
The joy would be encompassing.
Only yesterday, I searched an old picture of me for the
flaws I saw then,
flaws no longer apparent to my aged eyes.

The admission of longing gives me freedom,
of heart,
and mind,
and aged body.
I am set free by my own
permission to grieve,
not for the loss of youth,
but for the fact that I did not treasure it.

Dust Bowl

The dust rolls in to Kansas town
on waves of wind full bore from hell.
Spare growth on once prolific ground
lets blackness sweep across the plain.

No saint can save the fam'ly farm
from dust ten inches deep that chokes
the calf and child found side by side
and mother's cry cannot be heard

through roar of beast man made in time
to shatter poor and restless heart.
The orange glow above the cloud
at sunset tells its onward path

into the east, the dust storms on,
and men must factor nature's hand
into the plans for living there
where soil is lifted to the sky.

The huddled refugees embark
for storied California shores
where food and sun are common things
and dust is left to barren ground.

Ireland Bound

The dreary view along the cobble path
brings tears and wailing memories to mind
of troubles we were dragged and bound to bear.

It was an Ireland of home, and hearth, and warmth.
Flesh ground into resistance breaks the threshold.
A place we were to live becomes the place
we merely exist.

Green, green hills and mists
Run red with blood of kin, oh! my own blood.

Will conflict ever subside to calm?
Will the weary rest a sleep of battle-hardened dread,
or put their souls on shelves at night, next to brothers,
and mothers,
and enemies that live next door?

Bound by tradition, pride, and loyalty:
The stance has proved unmoving, and for what?
Dead boys in open spaces in the ground,
and holes in hearts that cannot weep their loss.

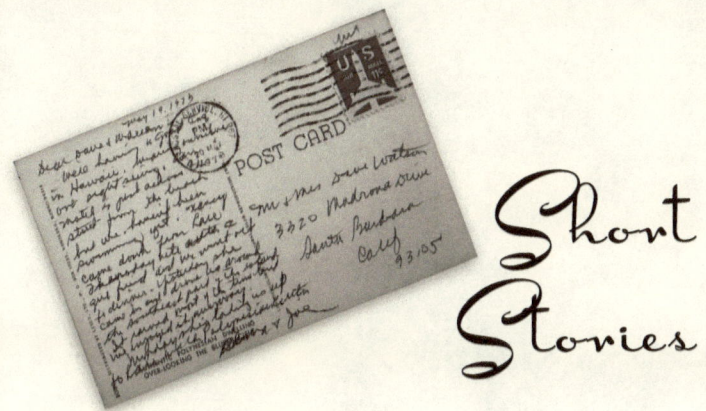

Short
Stories

Path Before Giants

*C*assiopeia appeared, low in the summer sky. I first saw her in my youth when I stood on the vast Dakota plain with a calf in my arms and tears smeared on my face. Daddy pointed up to the stars, telling me how Poseidon banished Cassiopeia to the heavens for selfishness. "She reminds us of our duty to those in our keep," he said. I looked on while Daddy took my sick calf and put it down.

I always searched for her. I oriented myself around the ancient constellation instead of the North Star, like the rest of mankind; her sweeping arc through the heavens showing me how I moved, how I changed, and I judged my derelictions against her willful breach. I was miles and years away from that little girl, but Cassiopeia's points of light still dictated her eternal repose. I wanted to be up there beside her.

Coffee warmed my hands, and I stretched my feet toward the fire, the flames an adversary to the slight chill of the mountain air. John sat next to me in our forest campsite, high up on a hill and overlooking a tall grass meadow. The stars fanned out below us over the tops of the distant trees and I felt peace at seeing her again.

Camping was never my favorite thing, but the parts I loved, the stars and the quiet of evening, would usually make up for sleeping on the ground and waking to the cold of early morning. I promised John long ago I would go with him wherever he wanted to go.

*I*n the morning, we decided to go for a walk among the trees of Calaveras Big Trees State Park. I was impressed on the drive into the campground, and up close, they were surely giants. The high canopy overhead was like a cathedral: bright, peaceful, inspiring worship.

We walked in silence, far apart but not distant, the kind of closeness in space that long marriage brought. We came to a trailhead that had markers and a delineated path, but the first thing on the trail was a stump of a tree. It was not the most encouraging start.

"The Big Stump," John read aloud.

"The Big Stump? Who named it that? Seems a little obvious. And why is a stump the beginning of a trail?"

John finished reading the marker at the base of the stump while I walked up the stairs and stood on the large expanse that was once the base of an enormous tree. "It is so large, a small building once sat atop it."

I could dance on it the way I danced at my wedding.

"Sequoiadendron giganteum." John read. Made it sound like a dinosaur. "The species has been traced back fifteen million years. It is the largest living thing on Earth.

Only fractions of one percent of the seeds ever germinate. It takes a specific water content, sunlight, and depth for the seed to sprout into a tender beginning that looks like a blade of grass. It is the sole species in the genus Sequoiadendron."

On day seventy-three I knew I would marry him.

I descended the stairs and we walked into the forest. I got dizzy when I put my head far back, trying to see the tops of the trees all around us, the full scope of height elusive. In the stillness, my breath sounded loud and even the slight elevation of roots beneath my feet had structure. We reached another marker and a majestic specimen stood before us. Blackened edges on the bark showed where a fire touched this giant, but he withstood the threat. "Look John, this tree is like us. Big and strong, scarred but still standing."

John continued his narration. "The Empire State Tree. In 1907, Galen Clark wrote: 'The bright cinnamon color of their immense fluted trunks, in strong contrast to the green foliage and dark hues of the surrounding forest, makes them all the more conspicuous and impressive. In their sublime presence a person is apt to be filled with a sense of awe and veneration, as if treading on hallowed ground.'"

On day four hundred fifty-two, I said yes.

We began to wander more than walk, our purpose of getting to the end lost in the detail of really seeing majesty up close. Ahead of us, two trees touched at their bases and the marker named them 'Mother and Son.' There was an invitation on the marker to touch the trees here. The others on the path were guarded by words and short barriers. The softness of the bark surprised me, and I petted it like a puppy, ran my hand slowly down, then back up and down again. "I wish I could be a tree."

John laughed. "Why?"

On day one thousand four hundred forty-seven, our son was born.

I didn't answer him about why I wished to be a tree, but right then, I did want to be part of them. We passed ferns and moss-covered stones, shoulders touching briefly now and then as we followed the path sedately.

"Really, why would you want to be a tree?" He looked at me like he did when we didn't know everything about each other. I walked a bit more before I answered, letting the seconds emphasize the words. I didn't want the timbre of complaint to overburden the idea.

"Everyone would see who I was; no hiding behind social customs, no worrying about hurting someone's feelings. Just me. Beautiful on the whole, even if up close the flaws show, soft on the outside, but ultimately strong because I stand with others." I said these reasons out loud because they were true and right.

There were other reasons I kept to myself. I knew they were not so generous.

I wouldn't have to go where I didn't really want to. I

wouldn't have a burden of duty to others. My child would always be close by.

John said nothing, just smiled and walked on. I wondered if he would like to be a tree.

After a few silent steps, I added softly, "I wouldn't have to change. I would always and forever be just that one thing, a tree."

He moved closer and put his arm around my waist. "But Julie, you would still have to grow."

Growth and change are not always the same.

Another giant loomed ahead, but this one lay on the forest floor. Broken. Dead. The path led beside and through The Father of the Forest. Though it fell hundreds of years ago, only the interior decayed. The resulting tunnel was large enough for me to walk through. John noticed graffiti carved into the strong outer bark and he sputtered with anger at the defacement of something so beautiful.

"How could someone write his name on this? Who'll care that they were here? They've ruined this wonderful tree."

As I stepped inside, the sounds around me were muffled. The bark soundproofed the tunnel and my ears felt deaf in the few seconds it took to walk through to the end. It was a strange and new sensation of a physical barrier, of something damped down over me, isolating me from the outside world. Communication silenced.

We buried our son on day seven thousand sixty-two.

I came out the other side. The world reached my ears

again. Wind blew through the leaves, and the scrunching of John's shoes on the path brought comfort after the silence.

"John, in a few hundred years, someone may think it's interesting. They won't be offended then. Remember the graffiti in the pyramids? You thought that was fascinating. Remember?"

He grumbled to himself, and all I caught was ". . . still not right."

The next stop on the path was in front of The Abraham Lincoln. It was mature when he was president and gave the Gettysburg Address. I thought of the rows of graves facing Lincoln that day and marveled at his ability to speak those words with such a weighted grief as the loss of his own two sons and the war of a nation hung over him.

"Rate of Growth," read John. "They continue to grow throughout their lifetimes. The oldest known currently is three thousand three hundred years old. The trees gain two feet of height per year for the first fifty to one hundred years. After that, their growth is outward and upward. Rings of one-half inch thickness are common."

"See Julie, always growing." His words were kind, not chiding. He seemed to know I was fragile. He took my hand and we continued on. Up ahead, I could see the path going through one of the trees. We walked a bit faster, and I fleetingly thought I might run. I saw two old women standing inside the tree, touching the sides tenderly. We stalled at the marker and read about The Pioneer Cabin Tree. "A hole was cut in the base of the tree in the 1850s for wagons to drive through."

I wanted to give the ladies privacy, not push in, and rush their enjoyment, but we couldn't help drifting in beside them; it was big enough for us all. As I passed them, I realized they were searching for something. Here, too, were names and dates scratched along the tunnel carved by hand over a hundred and fifty years ago. They touched the names, carefully going over each one as if it were Braille for their fingers to read. I stopped and asked one of them, "Are you looking for someone?"

"Yes, my great-grandmother, Louise Marsden. She traveled through here in 1882. She was just eleven and carved her name in the tree when her father wasn't looking. I wanted to find her."

I decided to help look. I was shorter by inches and so more easily inspected the names below. A few well-spent moments found "Marsden 1882" underneath my fingers. "Oh, here!" I called them over and the same gentle touch greeted this name.

"I just wanted to touch her again."

Like I touched Jared's name on the cold granite stone.

I left them. It was not my memory. I rejoined my husband, who was waiting patiently as always on the other side. "See John, someone loves the graffiti." I was pleased to be right, but not in my usual smugness. The sunlight danced down through the leaves.

His hand slipped into mine again and we walked together, as we had for so many years. Around a turn, we found three giants standing majestically before us. The marker named them: "The Three Graces. Aglaea (Beauty), Euphrosyne (Mirth), and Thalia (Good cheer)." We stepped back, side by side, and gazed from trunk to crown and back again.

I was humbled, amazed at these living things. They were graceful, beautiful, and strong; all the things I wanted to be. I looked at John and realized he was more full of grace than I. How could he be?

On day ten thousand two hundred fifty-two, the doctor said he didn't have much time.

I looked more closely at his face. "What?" he asked.

"Nothing. Just looking at you." I kissed him, silently thanking him for being strong.

As we wound our way along, a clearing opened up to show a section of tree that lay on its side, taller than our house. The marker proclaimed it was The Discovery Tree. "This is the first tree discovered in this grove and felled in 1853. The ring count gives an age of one thousand two hundred forty-four years."

This very tree started growing in the year six hundred nine. There were two hundred rings when Charlemagne ruled, six hundred when the Magna Carta was signed. It had nine hundred rings when Da Vinci painted, and a thousand when Shakespeare wrote.

I was left, again, searching for words, but this time

due to awe and not for calculated effect. I was captivated by the idea of discovering something so grand, something that was here all along, but not seen by human eyes, not acknowledged to the world. My reverence was profound in front of this tree, lying in repose.

It was day fourteen thousand six hundred.

John stood a few feet from me. "You know this is the tree to The Big Stump, right?"

"It is not!" I protested immediately. The idea took a moment to settle in. I peered down the length of the tree on its side and I saw, over there, the stump of its past. The Big Stump. "This is the same tree we saw when we first started on the path? But it looks so different from over here."

"We're just on the other side, nothing's different."

In the silence of the forest, I understood the faint whisper of meaning in my husband's words, calling me away from the stars and back toward Earth. Cassiopeia could wait. Maybe duty was service, and grief, and solemn watch, without regard for how it all turned out in the end. Self-recrimination didn't fulfill a duty to any-one. The tree's repose mirrored Cassiopeia's, but the tree didn't intend to be cut from its base. It merely happened.

My hand felt the tree in a different caress, newly aware of our common tie, and I breathed in the scent of the wood.

You May Die Tonight

She doesn't look ninety-two. She looks seventy-five. But I have my master bed list with me, and it says right here: 514B Jenny Andrews, ninety-two-year-old female. I check her name band, and sure enough, all the names and numbers match. She's awake; she smiles at me. Her gaze shows an alertness that reassures me. Satisfied there is no need for me to intervene to save her life, I turn to my left and extend my hand to the younger woman standing there.

"I'm Lisa, the Nursing Supervisor," I tell her. "She must have scared you."

She takes my hand with a clammy, stiff grip and hangs on. "I'm her daughter, Kathy. I was afraid that . . ."

Kathy had screamed "Help! Somebody help!" from her mother's hospital room.

Screaming gets a reaction in a hospital hallway. Ten people were in the room when I got there to find Mrs. Andrews awake, aware.

People don't often see the human body when it malfunctions. The pale, gray, ghastly color, telling me a patient is losing consciousness, is still distressing to me after years of nursing. Families who've never seen it get a rude and indelible visual when sickness invades their everyday lives.

The ER admitted Mrs. Andrews earlier today. Her doctor wants her here for a few days because her heart rate is too slow. It should equal her age, but it was thirty this morning, and she kept passing out at home. She scared her daughter, who summoned the requisite help, wanting everyone and everything to make the horrible look stop. Now, Kathy stands by her mother's bed, tiny beads of sweat clinging to her forehead.

The telemetry monitor catches every beat of her heart. A tech upstairs watches the monitor each minute of the day and night. Telemetry tells all, painting a picture on a little graph: regular, irregular, fast, or slow. I assume the gray, sweaty skin her mother got during an episode of a decelerated rate prompted her daughter to call for help.

Mrs. Andrews seems all right now. As I'm standing at the foot of her bed, the monitor tech calls me from upstairs with information that changes the situation. With this last episode, moments ago, the telemetry showed a ten-second run of Torsade's, a lethal heart rhythm, not a mere sinus rhythm, that has slowed to a snail's pace.

I must be clear with her about options for treatment if her heart goes sideways.

"Hi, Mrs. Andrews. How are you feeling?" I ask her this simple question to confirm she's alert and knows what's going on.

"Well, honey, I'm just fine. Did I do it again? I woke up, and there were all these people. I must have done it again?" She searches her daughter's face for confirmation and receives it with a simple nod. "Oh, I'm sorry to cause trouble. I didn't want to stay, but Kathy was so upset."

She explains why she is here, apologizing for taking our time, our care. I want to say I wished all our patients actually needed us, as she currently does. Instead, I step to the side of the bed and sit down near her feet.

Most of the time, nurses don't sit on the patient's bed; somehow, it's considered rude or unprofessional. I judge she's a no-nonsense kind of girl and will not mind. I'm right, she smiles. Her expression softens and her face is angelic.

"Mrs. Andrews, I need to ask you a few questions." I glance over at the few remaining staff and shoo them away with my powerful boss look. "I need to make sure you are with it and know what's going on today. You know your heart starts beating too slow to get enough blood to your brain, and that's why you pass out."

"Yes," she says, her eyes clear, voice steady.

"Do you know where you are and what day it is?"

"I'm in the hospital instead of at home and it's a Tuesday in January, but I forget the date." She again searches her daughter's face, not receiving eye contact yet.

Alert and oriented, check. She can make decisions for herself.

"Ma'am, since you just arrived in the hospital, we don't have an order from the doctor yet as to what you want done should your heart stop or your breathing stop. Have you thought about if you would like us to treat you?"

It's hard to phrase questions about death, and I've done a better job than today, but she takes no offense and answers, "Heavens no, child. I've been here long enough."

I love her succinct answer.

I look up at Kathy, hopeful her mother has an ally. Her eyes dart around the room, stopping at the IV pole, the TV, anywhere except her mother's or my face. She wrinkles her nose, and I notice the stale hospital smell I can ignore until body language or words demand I attend to the distinct Eau d'Hospital. Her cheeks are drawn and pale, jaw tight. She fiddles with a wadded-up tissue. She is not ready for what may come, even if her mother is.

"So, we'll ask your doctor to write a DNR order. That means Do Not Resuscitate. We won't shock you or put a tube down your throat, but we can keep you comfortable. I want you to tell your nurse if you have pain or shortness of breath; we can give you medicines and oxygen if you need it. I would usually wait for the doctor to tell you this, but your heart isn't just slowing down, it's abnormal. It's a bad thing. You may die tonight." I say it as gently as I can, but honest and clear words are best to avoid misunderstandings.

Her face registers no shock, no fear. When I am ninety-two, it will be hard to surprise me as well.

"You only had a few seconds of this bad heart rhythm, and then it corrected itself. I can't guarantee it will correct itself if it happens again tonight." I continue speaking to Mrs. Andrews, but the words are for them both. "The treatment for this rhythm, Torsade's, is shocking you. It may be fixable if we shock you. I want to make sure I understand; you are saying you don't want us to try to fix it."

She searches Kathy's face again, and instead of the usual plea for guidance scared patients make to their families, she says, "I know it's hard for you to watch, but it's what I want. I raised you to be considerate of others and to go through things not because they are easy but because they are right."

She turns back to me, voice steady, sure, joyful. "Yes, that's right."

I feel a surge of admiration for this strong and kind woman. I pray to have her grace at the end of my life.

"There is a medicine, magnesium, that can prevent a recurrence of the bad rhythm. How about if we try it? It just goes in your IV."

She smiles at me, and I get the idea she knows I'm trying to make myself and Kathy feel better, to feel we are doing something. I get a nod.

"We'll take off all this monitoring equipment so you can get some sleep tonight. Your doctor should be here in a little bit, and we'll ask him to give us orders to fit your wishes."

I remove the telemetry monitor, and Kathy takes a chair near the bed, her hands fluttering back and forth from her lap to her face, the tissue a sad and useless clump. I offer her a new box; she need not ask the one tissue to serve her all night. Her lips turn up at the corners. She still does not meet my eyes.

As I come out of the room with the telemetry in my hand, her nurse asks me, "Is her rhythm fixed already?"

"I fixed it by not looking at it anymore."

In return, I get a blank stare and realize this new, young nurse does not know what I mean.

"If she doesn't want us to shock her, I don't want my monitor tech to watch it all night," I explain.

I call the physician at his office and tell him her wishes. He knows her well and gives me the orders I need to keep her comfortable and treat her heart conservatively. He says he'll be in to see her within the hour. Physicians should hear DNR wishes directly from the patient.

For the rest of the evening, Kathy and her mother visit. Soft voices and laughs drift out into the hall, and we know they enjoy each other. They are playing their parts in a dramatic moment in their lives, taking in all the lasts. Kathy stays the whole time, sleeping in the chair. I check them in the early hours of the new day, but now they are quiet, blankets up around their chins. I stand in the doorway, the lights not bright enough to show their faces. They are still, and I can hear their breathing. I'm not needed.

A few hours later, Kathy appears at my office door. Her eyes are wet with tears, and I know her mother has left her, but the panic has left her too. She had the chance to spend the last few hours in a way few experience. Her mother could have spared her the grief, for a while, but she would have robbed her of the opportunity to greet the end of life with dignity and grace. Her eyes meet mine with silent thanks.

I watch Kathy walk away down the hall, adjusting her posture as if she's hearing her mother reminding her to walk straight and tall. I watch her until she turns the corner, then I go in to listen to Mrs. Andrew's chest and her not beating heart.

Karl

I boarded the bus and handed the driver my money. "I want to find Karl," I said, hoping I didn't sound crazy.

He gave me the friendly-to-the-tourists smile and said, "Yah, Mon. We find him."

Seventy-eight humid degrees in Jamaica, the early October morning still snuggling in bed with Katie, I left to seek the artist in Negril who had a local reputation as a Master. I took my seat, left side near the window, and fixed my eyes on the horizon, letting the patchwork of buildings blur into a single streak of color. His name was Karl; that's all I knew for sure. He lived somewhere in town, but no one could give me an address. He only worked now if you asked him yourself, or so they said.

My wife wanted a painting of herself: a portrait. I came to this conclusion shortly before we left for Jamaica. She had seemed distant, unhappy. When I asked her what was wrong, she denied in words the absence of joy, but her face and actions showed sadness in a subtle way. One entire wall of her office was a corkboard, which held magazine pictures of people and places, strong women, and words. She collected words. A writer would do such a thing, but she clipped them out and pinned them up. Different fonts, different words, as if the right one would fit a place in her heart where something was missing.

She offset her constant collecting by using what she found. In her dreamy prose, forged but recognizable, appeared the words and images amassed in her search for a unique voice. She wrote often and read her stories to me in the evening while we shared a dessert. I tried to interpret her from the clues she left on the wall, certain that whatever had been bothering her was hanging there, only I couldn't pick it out and feared she would fail me like a schoolboy for not getting it in time. Strong women in various poses showed up in a recurrent theme and I felt glee when I decided she must want a portrait. I would surprise her and win her back; find the piece her heart needed.

We stopped in front of a shantytown area—crooked walls and patched roofs, more poverty than artistry, but the driver nodded his head at my unspoken question.

"Fifth place down on the right, red paint with a porch." Smiling a more sincere smile this time, he added, "Evry 'ting Irie."

I got out, handed him a good tip; I wanted him to come back for me after I acquired my prize.

I walked down the dirt road, counting the shacks

where the artists showed their work. They shouted to each other; friendly calls of "Yah Mon" carried on the heavy island air. The smell of red clay and the warm, blanketing breeze made me feel at home in a place I'd never been.

Fifth place down, right side. There he was, sitting on the porch, with a young boy at his feet. Together, all knees and elbows, they appeared the contrast of age, one of coltish growth, one of waning might.

"Are you Karl?" I asked.

"Yah, Mon, I'm Karl. Whatch you want?" He turned toward the sound of my voice, and from the few feet that separated us, I saw the gray cataracts that covered both his eyes.

"Uh, Um, Uh . . ." I stuttered as my mind raced. A blind painter? They sent me to a blind painter. How is a blind painter going to paint a portrait of my wife?

I fell silent, arms at my sides, defeated before I began. The young boy got up from his place and came to stand in front of me. The top of his head barely reached my elbows, and he had to tilt his head back to look up into my face.

"Karl paint for you," he said. "I mix the paint for him, but he still as good as when he could see. Come and look." He motioned me into the darkened shack, waving his hand. "Start here."

He directed my attention to the right side of the room, and I stood facing the wall, waiting for my eyes to adjust to the dim light. Portraits hung and sat and tipped all along the wall. Black, White, Asian, Indian faces, rendered in all the colors of the rainbow that described humanity. My eyes made a slow sweep to the back and left. I didn't need to step in any direction. The room was small. The young boy busied himself at my left hand, telling me about all the paintings and Karl's great talent, which I could see for myself. "Show me something he's done recently," I said, afraid that the boy would bring out something garish and unclear.

"Here," the boy pointed to a small collection, set aside on the left. "Dey dry here."

I drew in a quick breath, realizing I had failed to consider the fact that a painting would have to dry. I would not be able to take it to Katie today. The boy misinterpreted my noise as delight, and he squirmed about, smiling, eyes shining while he showed off the pieces as though we were in a museum instead of a dirty, sad little shack. My cool hesitation began to melt as I looked at these newer works. They were a bit more impressionistic, more Van Gogh than Rembrandt, but the likenesses were real, and the colors vivid. The portraits seemed alive.

"So, you want Karl to paint for you?" The boy looked less like a little beggar and more like an usher, sure of where he was placing me.

"Yes, please. I want a portrait of my wife." The words fell unbidden from my mouth, but once aloud, they became a true petition.

The boy brought an easel to where Karl was sitting and he scurried about, getting the paints and brushes ready. Karl felt for the canvas and looked toward his workspace. No doubt he could make out shapes, light, and some color, but I was unable to imagine how he could paint. He directed me with pointed finger and a nod of his head to sit on the porch rail in front of him.

"Tell me about her," Karl requested.

"I have a picture." I offered it to the boy. He took it to Karl and moved it around his visual field until Karl turned away, satisfied.

"Tell me about her." he said again.

I described my wife's features, thinking that he hadn't been able to visualize her from the picture. "She has blond hair, five feet six inches tall. Square face and rounded nose. Blue eyes with long lashes. She smiles a lot."

Karl laughed low. "No Mon, tell me about her. Tell me who she is, what she loves. Dat's how I paint now. I paint the spirit, not the flesh. Those t'ings are the black and white of people. Color comes from inside."

I shoved both hands deep into the pockets of my jeans, as if there I could find a single item to show him—this is her, this is how I feel, this is who she is. My arms hugged my sides and protected the part of me that feared I did not know her well enough. I started again, the words at first no more descriptive than arched brow and soft skin, but I soon found my hands in the air, showing him in blurred gestures the way she spoke with her whole body, her hands expressive and charming.

I defined her as he painted. Much the way I looked at her workspace for clues as to who she was, and what she needed, I gave him bits and pieces that became, altogether—her. She loved music and poetry, could speak four languages to my one, and intrigued me daily, even after fourteen years. She threw her head back when she laughed and cooked in stocking feet and a black apron, with a glass of merlot in her hand. Katie made funny faces in the mirror when she put on her mascara and made funny faces at me in the middle of an argument to make me laugh.

I mimicked her voice and manner of speech while Karl painted. He would stop to listen, or perhaps think of something from before his eyes had failed him. I unburdened my mind by telling him of her strength and kindness and wit, filling in the shape, the shadow, the highlight that was Katie. He worked steadily, interrupting sometimes for a detail of her face, or requesting a color from the boy.

"Mix pink like the lady near the mirror and a red like the dancing girl." Karl spoke kindly to the boy, in a low and steady tone like the warmth of the island air. "Terrence is my nephew, my sister's boy," he said to me as the boy disappeared into the dark. I realized that each time he needed a color, he qualified it, and they were the colors of his previous portraits.

"Why you come to Jamaica, Mon?" Karl asked after we fell silent for too long.

"For vacation, to make her happy. Katie's been, I don't know, distant lately. People change over the years and who's to say that because you're married, you change along the same paths? I've asked her what's wrong, and she doesn't know. She says she's not unhappy. I thought getting away, being able to pay attention to her, would help."

"Yah Mon?" Karl's eyebrows lifted high on his forehead.

"She seems content. I'm just worried. I don't want to realize someday that I've lost her."

"Whatch you want from her, your Katie?"

His question caught me by surprise. "I want her to be happy, I guess."

"No Mon, that's whatch you want *for* her. I asked whatch you want *from* her."

"Nothing. Just love. Love and understanding."

"So. Maybe that's all she want from you too."

His words crept in, simple words that held meaning I barely caught, knowing there was more depth than my instinctive defense allowed. "But I do love her and understand her."

"Is not the same, lovin' and understandin'. Love is some'tin you do. Understandin' is some'tin you give."

How simple to say. How difficult to remember the way to do it. He left me to my quiet thought. I wanted to repair whatever was wrong in Katie's world, assuming it must have something to do with me. I was so concerned with how I felt about it, I had failed to simply love her and give her the understanding she needed for whatever it was that made her seem so far away. I looked at Karl with a rush of gratitude. A blind man saw my life more clearly than I did, yet he didn't judge. He just led me to see it clearly again myself.

And then he was finished. It was her. I touched his shoulder to let him know I wanted to shake his hand, to thank him for his work in a way that money never could. I was afraid to speak, sure he would hear the tears on my face.

"Tomorrow. Come back tomorrow, Mon. It be dry enough den. Bring Katie which'you?" Karl smiled toward me, shaking my hand and feeling the nod in my grip.

On the twenty-minute ride back to the hotel, past businesses, more shantytowns, and beachfront houses, I saw things differently. They were all just things, the black and white of people.

When I entered the room, Katie wasn't there, and her sunglasses and beach bag were gone. I knew where to find her.

I changed quickly, not knowing if we would end up in the water, but we usually did. Katie seemed to love it more than land. I tripped twice, trying to get my foot into the board shorts and make my way to the door at the same time.

I jogged down to the beach, seven miles of white sand meeting blue water, so perfect it looked in real life like it did in the pictures. The eastern border of the resort as my starting point, I walked in the surf line, acting as if I were savoring the beach, when in fact I was worried my eyes were red, and I wanted more time to compose what I would say. I scanned the people as I passed, looking for Katie, wanting to glimpse her from far away so I could watch her for a while before she recognized my Pennsylvania tan and unruly hair. I let myself enjoy the little wavelets lapping at my feet. If I closed my eyes, I could not tell them from bath water.

I saw her, finally, from a hundred feet away and I smiled, knowing how she would greet me. Completely trusting, welcoming, no question in her mind of subversion. She would be eager to hear my story. I was lucky that way. I was lucky in countless ways. Katie sat reading in the now hot October sun, holding a happy orange drink, tipping her head back to see out from under the brim of her sunhat.

"Where've you been?" She waved and pulled her glasses off. She always took them off when we spoke.

"I went looking for something for you, to make you happy, and instead I found something from you."

She cocked her head to the side and took a sip from her drink, savoring the moment of suspense. "I didn't know I was so powerful. What'd I get you?"

"Understanding." I couldn't say much more.

"It fits." Her smile told me more than the words. She held out her hand. "Let's go swimming."

We walked slowly toward the water, and she ran her hand up my arm, patting it lightly in reassurance. I assumed she was speaking words that did the same and barely caught the last few. She said, "Did you know your shorts are on backwards?"

She threw her head back in laughter as my panicked face gave away my hurry to dress. I didn't want to look down to see my embarrassment, but when I did, I found the tie strings in perfect order. My dismay gave way to relieved giggles, and I stood there, love-struck and laughing, watching Katie run full tilt into the bluest water in the world.

Serengeti, May 2001

*D*ear Stella,

Jambo! Your father and I flew here from Arusha this morning. We had to buzz the landing strip because there were so many zebras. They scattered like oil in water. You really could see the Masai villages from the air, although we didn't fly very high the whole trip. Two thousand, three thousand feet maybe? We left early when the sun was just rising to beat the afternoon thunderstorms. I don't mind the rain. It's pretty to listen to, and it makes the tsetse flies go away for a bit. You were right. They can bite right through my jeans.

We did a game run when we first arrived and saw lions right away. Leopard have been more difficult to see but Patrick—you remember him—says to look for their tails hanging down from the branches of the sausage trees.

Your descriptions have been perfect. It's odd that now we are here where you live and study, and you are home in New York. I wish you could have joined us for fun. Patrick is excellent, though, and he speaks fondly of you. Is he your interpreter for the Masai, or does he have another role with the university?

I'm sure your Kiswahili is better than mine. Patrick smiles at my feeble attempts to direct him when we are out on the savannah. I've got the names of the animals down, but oh, the directions! I say stop when I mean go and I just have it all backwards.

I'm starting to understand why you love it here. When I stepped off the plane, I had this sudden sense of home. I've never felt anything like it, anywhere. Nothing is the same, not the animals, the plants, the smells, the weather. And yet, it somehow feels familiar and comfortable. At least I think I understand why you rarely come home. I would live here if I could.

I am writing this while sitting under a gazebo near the pool at the hotel. It's a very nice place and I love how it is hidden around the back side of a hill so you can't see it from the plain. I noticed there are no contrails above us. And it is so quiet. Peaceful quiet, not something-is-wrong quiet. I can hear the bugs, whatever they are, singing in the tall grass, and the Wildebeest have that honking bray that travels a long way. The giraffe sneak up on you, though, because they don't make a sound, and then suddenly you turn a corner and there they are!

It's still raining a little and just now a rather large male baboon has come up to the pool to drink. He's sitting across the water from me, and I am out here by myself. Let's see, you said don't make eye contact, sit still, and do not move or threaten him. Is this what pretty young girls in bikinis at a Las Vegas pool feel like?

He's moved on now. I admit, I was a little anxious. I haven't felt like I was in danger at all so far, even when we were just feet from the lion. The only time my heart raced was when we first arrived in-country and the men at the Nairobi airport pulled your father out of the line for customs and questioned him because they said he looked like a drug dealer. Can you imagine? Evidently, males with blond hair are drug dealers. Females with blond hair are fascinating.

That would be you, my blond darling. Fascinating. Do they touch your hair a lot? Patrick says the Masai will want to touch my hair. I don't know how long you are planning to be in New York, but please let's go to Windows on the World when we get back. You used to love going there. We'll be here for another two weeks and then your father has business in Istanbul, so I'll go with him there and then I don't know after that. I'm sure we'll be back in New York in late June.

It's tearing me apart to be so far away from you and to never see you at all. Please make an effort to meet us in New York. Please? You can even bring your friend, Jennifer. Or is it Jessica? I'm sorry I haven't written it in my address book. I'll make sure your father is on his best behavior and we'll have a very nice dinner and visit.

It's getting dark and I can hear the hyena off in the distance, so I better go back to the room. Your father will wonder what's kept me. I'll be waiting to hear that you will still be in New York when we return. I miss your voice and I miss the way you raise your eyebrows when you don't agree with me, as you are likely doing right now. Maybe you can stay in New York until October. It will be Homecoming then and Trey Williams' mother said he'd be home for a week or so. He was always sweet on you. Anyway, just a thought.

Love you, my dear darling girl,
Mother

Constant Weight

The remainder of Cassie came in the mail, to her own front door, in a plain white plastic box. She was small and dense. Scott closed the front door and carried her to the living room, measuring her heft, lifting the box up and down. She was so slight a few weeks ago, the last time he carried her. He situated her on the couch and positioned himself on the adjacent cushion, adding his weight so she did not tip over. Plastic was not reverent enough for what was left of his heart, but it was practical.

"Where'd I put your pretty wood box?" he asked Cassie. She didn't answer.

He traced the rim of the box with his finger, circumscribing her completely in the amount of space he used to trace a circle on her stomach as they lay in bed. Months ago. Cassie asked once if he'd still do that when she had a scar.

He stood and walked to their bedroom, past the cards standing open on top of the piano like kindergarteners in line. He lay down for a moment on the unmade bed, toes still touching the wood floor as if there were cinder blocks tied to his feet. He traced circles in the space next to him.

The dog nudged him on the hand that touched Cassie's side and he met Abby's eyes while he woke. She was the best dog ever. Lines on his arm showed the tangle of sheets, imprinted by deep and motionless sleep. He stumbled to the closet and waited for a hint as to why he was there. He caught the scent of gardenias on her long gray sweater, patted the sleeve and held it to his face, resting his cheek on the soft cashmere. To the left of her sweater, on the shelf below her perfumes and the tin-bordered mirror, with her wedding dress and their love letters tied up in a burgundy ribbon, sat the small, burled wood box he'd bought two days after her death. Cremation allowed procrastination. He didn't know what to do with her still.

In the living room, he opened the wood box first, preparing to transfer her from temporary new body to permanent new body. The lid of the mailing container popped up without much force and inside was a bag with a metal twist tie and a round metal tag, like a dog tag, with "Chastain—January 20, 2013" stamped into it.

"I should have touched you more."

He opened the bag and put his finger into it, down far enough to touch her, then brought it up to his tongue and brushed it with the sandy ash. No taste, no smell. She felt gritty when he expected a powdery softness and he rolled her between his fingers, letting her fall back into the bag. It didn't mean anything, touching the remains. It wasn't her, anyway. He retied the bag and placed her in the wood box via a hidden panel in the bottom and tightened the screw to seal it.

He made a space for her among the condolence cards on the piano, but the arrangement looked too much like an altar. Ashes on the mantle looked better, but it wasn't quite wide enough, and he didn't want her to fall and spill onto the carpet. He would have to vacuum her up, mixing her with the dog hair and dirt from the garden. He settled on the sideboard in the formal dining room. He could see it from the kitchen, but he didn't ever sit at the lovely teak table Cassie bought three years ago. Abby sat near her, staring at the box, and turning to look at him standing in the kitchen as if to say, "Do you know she's in this box?"

In the weeks after her funeral, people who looked familiar asked how he was doing and said, "We're sorry for your loss." He counted the times he felt repulsed by Cassie's scar and when he passed ten, he knew he was superficial and shallow.

Roses hung from a hook near the laundry room door, blackened by the years since Cassie cut and tied them with raffia. She scattered roses and gardenia throughout the house like a Monet painting. He kept the tied roses even though they were not the alive version. Cassie wasn't the alive version either.

Cassie's best friend, Anna, came over on Sundays and Thursdays. She listened to his rants and sat silent when he sobbed. Cassie moved around the house as the weeks went by. On a Thursday morning when Cassie was again on the piano, Anna rang the bell and roused him from a fretful sleep to join her at Bible Study. Glory to God in the Highest. They talked about making daily lists and writing down prayer to prompt change and healing. He promised to make a list.

"Let's see it," Anna said as he opened the door on Sunday.

"See what?"

"The list—you know—from Bible Study?"

"Oh."

She followed him into the kitchen, and he slid it across the counter to her.

get up

feed dog

make coffee

"That's it?"

"Yep."

"Needs a little work."

Anna reached for two cups in the left-hand cabinet, kept her back to Scott and poured creamer in hers and coffee in both, adding a little at a time to make them even. "She was my best friend too. You cannot check out—you have to find a new life."

"I don't want a new life, thank you," he said, as if

refusing an offer of going to a play or the beach. He said the same thing about the funeral. It happened anyway.

"I'm going to wear my red bra when I see him," Cassie said, smiling at Scott in the mirror, catching his eye over her shoulder. *"It's spread, they think. I'll go tomorrow to talk to him in his office. We'll go."*

At the funeral, Anna asked the mourners to write about a memory of Cassie, and as he watched them drop the notes into a box near her casket, the small gestures they made toward her felt like they were stabbing her instead, and his chest wouldn't let the air come in.

Some days were still crushing like the funeral, but for these past few months, he gave himself ten minutes in the morning to cry. The all-day tears were exhausting. And yet, some days, her pillow didn't move from under his head, rendered flat by the constant weight of grief.

The next Sunday, he added to the list.

Get up

Feed the dog

Make coffee

Groceries

Dust

Prune the roses

Find a place for Cassie

Anna found the list lying on the counter next to a box of raspberry coffee cake.

"Your list has changed," she said.

"I can't find a place in the house that seems normal."

"Do you want her somewhere besides the house? A place you can visit?"

"But the ashes aren't her. She's here, not there." Scott pointed to himself as the place Cassie was.

"Then where will you scatter her?"

"I don't know." He shoved his hands into his pockets and rocked back and forth.

"Are you ready to read the notes from the funeral?" Anna asked the question every Sunday. He'd never said yes.

Scott got up and retrieved the notes from their place in the closet.

Anna sat on the couch and patted the cushion next to her. Scott sat, elbows on knees, hands clasped, shielding his belly and heart.

"Maybe we'll find an answer in the notes." Anna was always positive. He hated it at the moment.

The notes were blah and then crushing, comforting, and irritating all at the same time. He didn't want to hear the words, but Anna's voice filled the quiet with memory. The notes did not answer his question. It had never come up in all the things Cassie talked about. It was like forgetting the centerpiece on a party table. Not essential, but always the finishing touch. She requested cremation, and he failed to ask where she would like to be afterwards.

Anna put down the note box. "Maybe she'd like to be everywhere?"

"You mean small amounts in different places?"

"Yeah, like a pilgrimage. Or delivery service." Anna grinned.

"Not all at once like putting her in the ground."

"Precisely. That's your list for next week."

The next Sunday he told Anna the few places he could recall. Together they listed new destinations and discussed the pros and cons of both what they thought Cassie would like, and the logistical challenges to skirting the laws against scattering human remains. It was only tiny amounts. They planned for a week off their respective jobs, accounted for weather, and chose the last week in September, three weeks away.

Early on the first day, they put Cassie on the ottoman and spent an hour sifting her into small pill bags. They only needed twelve but packed fifteen, just in case. They placed her into a jewelry box with a hinged lid and she rode between them in Scott's truck console.

In Yosemite, Cassie was caught up in a gust of mountain air when Scott opened the small bag and tipped it, not thinking that the breeze would carry her from the base of the tree he chose. He freed her with greater care at Calaveras Big Trees State Park, and she settled at the feet of giant sequoias, their fluted trunks towering to the sky and watching over her. She floated down the river at Sutter's Mill, and he watched her flow, then eddy, then race over a rock until she dispersed too much to follow the water that carried her.

Lake Tahoe's deep blue water held her in an ancient embrace. Cassie entered the Pacific Ocean at The Golden Gate Bridge, mixing with the jade green water that flowed into and out of the bay. She loved the gardens at Mission San Juan Bautista, and they spread her under a rose bush between the statue of Saint John the Baptist and the church built in 1797.

Anna and Scott walked on Moonstone Beach. He stared at his feet, making impressions in the sand while Anna looked for places further out.

"You know," Anna said, "grief makes you look short term, like looking down at your feet."

Scott straightened and considered her, walking more than arm's length, but beside him. He appreciated her intuitive sense of his space. "And if I look up?"

"Then you'll see further down the road. I could always pick out my way when I could see exactly where I was going. Broad daylight, full moon, low tide. Remember to look up sometimes."

They took Cassie to El Capitan State Beach for the summers she spent there, and to Malibu, because who wouldn't want to be there for eternity? They scattered her near the H in the Hollywood Sign, then headed to Griffith Observatory where Cassie went to a junior astronomy camp. Some nights in the summer when she was sick, Scott would find her out on the chaise in the yard with the blue and green blanket over her thin legs, lying back and staring at the stars. Anna sat with him on a bench on the walkway to the Observatory and watched the sun go down and the stars peek out. Los Angeles glittered below, and they scattered Cassie near the bust of James Dean, below Venus in the evening sky.

The Lily Pond at Balboa Park was last on the list and was crowded with visitors.

"Should I pretend I'm looking at the fish?" he asked as they sat on one of the cadre of benches on either side of the pond, meant for reflecting on something other than how to sneak ashes into the water.

"What if you poured her into your hand, so it doesn't look like you're emptying the bag? Then just lightly touch the water and she'll be gone." Anna made a graceful pass in the air with her hand.

Scott knit his eyebrows at the last word.

"Sorry, I meant she would float into the water off your hand. I'm sure lots of people touch the water."

"Like washing my hands of her." It was logical. He hated it. He let her float as the Carillion chimed noon.

The house felt the same when he returned. Empty, sad. An even smaller remainder of Cassie sat on the sideboard in the formal dining room, in case he needed her. He'd left the bag of ashes out of the wood box, thinking he'd know what to do by the time he returned. He put the bag in her gray sweater pocket, and she hung in the closet for a day or two until he bumped into her getting his tie from the rack and felt disrespectful, like he'd bumped into her in the subway. Scott pulled her out of the pocket and walked around the house with her, asking her where the last of her would like to be.

The scattering hadn't brought him peace. It was so useless. All of it. Her dying, her ashes going to places that were beautiful and fitting as a final resting place, when she would prefer being useful.

The smell of gardenias came in through the French door in the bedroom when he found himself back where he started. He could see the glossy green leaves and white flowers that always surprised him with their softness; because they looked like porcelain, he expected them to be hard and cold. He stepped onto the brick patio and reached to touch the blossoms, petted the velvet petals like he stroked Cassie's hair on the night of her diagnosis. There were only two gardenias now where there had been three, the one nearest the door a casualty of moving day when the burly men crushed the delicate branches as they brought the hospital bed through the wide open white doors.

Cassie would like a new gardenia here.

He dug the hole like the picture on the tag from the nursery. Then he tested the pH to make sure it was less than 7.0 and amended the soil with peat moss and Cassie. He placed the plant in the hole, careful to leave the roots undisturbed, and watered it, letting it drink until the soil was moist and dark brown.

He stood up, back aching from bending over and lifting the heavy plant. Water from the hose washed the loose dirt from his hands and he set all the tools back in their spots before going into the bedroom.

He lay down on the bed, the smell of gardenias drifting into his sleep, Cassie resting and useful not so very far away.

Angel Coin

*I*t felt like earthquake weather; the evening air was sticky and calm, rare in Central California. Full moons grabbed all the glory for being harbingers of busy nights but earthquake weather was worse.

My phone rang the second I put it in my scrub pocket after report from the day supervisor: ER needed supplies, med surg needed me to look at a post-operative patient. The OR crew was there late with an older woman who needed emergency surgery for a ruptured bowel. So I sped through the easy tasks and was ready when they moved her to the ICU after seven hours of surgery and asked me to find the daughter and bring her into the unit.

I managed high-stress, high-grief situations often. I was the nursing supervisor, the administrator on duty, responsible for the entire building and everyone in it. With this much responsibility, I had no direct patient care and few routine tasks. Every shift, I walked ten miles and interacted with countless staff and patients. Sometimes I brought bad news to those least able to deal with it. Nurses live countless experiences through the patients they care for, privileged to attend birth and death and life traumas in between. Those traumas burdened my heart.

I felt in the bottom of my scrub pants pocket, trying to find the pewter angel coin I always carried whenever I entered the hospital for a shift. I had a few of the coins and would give them away to my nurses sometimes, but never to patients or family. It was a touchstone of sorts; it helped me feel connected to my son and husband when I was on the house. I rarely saw my son in the morning before he dressed in his polo shirt and khaki shorts and ran the two blocks to school. He told the teacher I slept all day when his class discussed what parents did for a living. I touched the coin and asked the angel for strength, and for guidance too.

I brought the daughter into the ICU so she could sit in a rigid, uncomfortable chair at the foot of her mother's bed. The nurses moved like waves back and forth, touching her mother's skin, her face, then moving away toward the sound of an infusion in need of attention. I listened to her mother's heart and lungs, counted the cycles of breathing and pumping, and listened to the fluid gurgle near her back. The ICU nurses hung blood to replace her losses and checked the central line pressures, writing the numbers all together in a chart that showed the ebb and flow of her life. Small talk is different in a room where your mother is dying. The daughter told us she loved her garden and so we talked to her mother about peppers and tomatoes while the ventilator breathed in and out.

The surgeon stayed for two or three hours while we stabilized her a bit. No runs of tachycardia, no precipitous drops in blood pressure. We weaned the dopamine to a much lower dose than she tolerated before. At about two in the morning, the surgeon went home to sleep.

Usually at night in our sixty-four bed hospital there was only one doctor in house, the ER doctor. I stayed in the ICU, my presence and clinical experience a comfort to the staff. My hands were an extra set of essential tools. We turned the mother to move the wet and bloodied sheets out from under her, replacing them with clean ones. As we smoothed her hair on the pillow, she went into cardiac arrest.

We opened the fluids wide, gave her epinephrine and atropine, and checked the breathing tube placement. I explained what was happening while we did CPR. The ER doctor appeared within three minutes and took over running the code. The daughter stayed. I explained that her mother's body couldn't overcome the loss of ten feet of dead bowel the surgeon told her he removed. We worked for a half hour or so, using every drug and treatment in the algorithm, then looked to the daughter for permission to stop.

She nodded yes, tears running freely. We looked to the clock and called out a time. Everyone trickled out of the room except for me.

I sat near the daughter, to answer questions or just be there—but she asked no questions. I felt an incredible sadness from her, and I was compelled to give her my angel coin. I reached in my pocket and pulled it out. I handed it to her and said, "I hope you don't mind. I think she would want you to have this."

She looked down at the coin and wailed. I immediately feared I gave the wrong person my angel. I patted her shoulder and said nothing as she began to shake. I steeled myself for the wrenching sobs, but instead what came was laughter. She took in a great big breath and threw her head back, tears still running freely. I thought she was hysterical. Sometimes people laugh at inappropriate times. She wiped her face and sat up straight.

"Mom said she'd be my guardian angel if she died before me! That's just like her to figure out how to remind me right away. Thank you."

We brushed her mother's hair, and the daughter covered her with clean sheets for her last trip. I added another line weight to my heart.

Two years later, a new charge nurse started working on med surg. She was smart, hardworking, and kind. I liked going to her unit when she was there. She told me she wanted to make a difference. So many of us did.

On a rare and sweetly slow evening, I went to her unit and sat in the office, poured coffee, and we talked about how nursing was not what we expected, but better in some ways as well. I was moved to give one of my angel coins to my new friend. She looked at the distinct angel and almost fell off her chair.

"It was YOU!" she exlaimed. She began crying and talking so fast that I couldn't understand her or tell if she was happy or angry.

"What did I do?"

"It was you. You gave my friend this coin when her mom died."

She knew the story. I never told anyone I gave away my angel coin, somehow afraid it would be seen as "unprofessional."

"I've only given that to one family. Was she mad?"

"No, no. You don't understand. She thought it was the perfect thing. She had the angel tattooed behind her ear so she would always have it with her. That story is what made me want to be a great nurse, to make a difference in someone's life. It was you."

I experienced a profound rush of gratitude, happiness, and deep satisfaction. Gratitude for the story coming back to me, like a hawk to my arm, an unseen tether between me and my actions, happiness at knowing I made a difference to someone, and satisfaction that my desire to make a difference was perpetuated like ripples across a clear blue lake. It was a random, spontaneous act of kindness and it changed at least two lives. Then it changed mine.

Nursing and medicine are often seen as successful

only if we save a patient. This redefined success for me. I saw the bigger picture of life, not just the close-ups of illness and injury that weighted my heart. The daughter was touched by my gesture, and that was enough to make the difference I imagined.

I stopped letting those in my care break my heart. I spent years adopting grief in my attempts to console, but no patient or family asked it of me. In fact, they had no idea I carried their sorrow too. Proof I made a difference, at least once, showed me I didn't need to take on sadness to convince myself that I cared. I changed the very core of my interactions, and I began to see the world through this focused lens. I reached out to let patients and family know they were not alone, then stepped back from their pain and did not carry it with me anymore—the angel coin in my pocket a gentle reminder that I already made a difference.

Waiting

Nineteen seventy-five fluttered to the floor from pages of *The Prophet* when Catie pulled wisdom and advice from the bookcase to use as a coaster. She bent over to pick up the stray paper and recognized her own fifth-grade handwriting.

"I'm waiting for her to die. If she makes me wear the 'I'm a PIG' bib one more time, I'm going to help her out somehow. So what, I spill a few things off my plate. I'm only ten. Do I really have to wear a baby bib that calls me a barn animal? Then she makes me go to my room for calling her a heathen. I asked Daddy why she's so mean, and he said she got kicked in the head by a horse once. I'm waiting for her to just die already."

Catie smiled at her younger self and the inflated, righteous indignation expressed against the woman who occupied her mind back then. The Step Monster.

Getting kicked in the head could certainly cause aberrant behavior, memory loss, and motor malfunctions. It did not, however, explain why a woman who agreed to love and honor and cherish a man as his wife loathed his child.

The Step Monster professed a love for sewing, so Daddy let her make all Catie's clothes. The seventies produced a vast fashion wasteland and pants with fish on them and yellow ball fringe on the bottom cried out an open invitation to social torture; fifth graders dished out ostracism, which stuck, and name calling that lasted until Catie punched Harold Rayburn in the mouth and made him cry.

It would have tempered the frumpy clothing if The Step Monster loved to cook. She was Polish. She boiled everything and made a dish called Kapusta that looked like vomit. Catie said she'd rather eat dog food and so ended up eating kibble from a bowl on the floor, with "I'm a PIG" already in place around her neck.

A litany of foods populated the list of things Catie couldn't eat anymore and when eating disorders became news in the eighties, she completely understood their genesis. She still gagged at even the idea of lima beans, served for a whole month straight after she snuck a handful of the beans into a napkin. But oh, the powdered milk, not mixed all the way and choked down in clumps, the worst of the food bastardizations. Most of the time, it came back up. She had to drink it over and over until it stayed down. It took three or four tries most of the time. Every single day.

Catie avoided her grasp, hands like pincers without softness or warmth. The Step Monster's skin was not even human, white and hard and cold like the toilet bowl. If Catie accidentally touched it, she rushed to wash her hands with hot water and scrub her nails with the little brush perched on the edge of the bathtub, where she took a bath once a week. Her school pictures well documented her embarrassing, greasy hair.

The Step Monster wore horn-rimmed glasses and a smirk, and her nasal, taut voice commanded in a never-ending loop, "You're grounded! Go to your room!"

Catie spent hours alone, forced to sit with a pacifier in her mouth for sucking her thumb, an accusation that came any time her hands neared her face, brushed aside a stray hair, or leaned on her palm when she watched TV. Catie cried stupid tears every time. During one of these exiles, she decided each hour spent should be an hour taken off The Step Monster's life.

When the Step Monster left Daddy in search of a feminist path on a sweltering Texas night in August of 1976, Catie rejoiced.

Mrs. Ina Dell came from the nursing home across the street at three thirty a.m. Rain outside came in with the medics, wrested from sleep, resigned to bring in the dross of calls. No fierce trauma or scary heart attack. She was hot and dry, probably septic and dehydrated. The skilled facility couldn't administer the necessary IV antibiotics and a DNR allowed the staff to move more calmly than if they were actively saving her.

On this Tuesday morning in February, no other patients waited or occupied treatment rooms, so Catie gave full attention to the slight form on the gurney in ER 5, a trauma bay with a door. She dimmed the lights and shut out the rest of the ER, then put a wet washcloth on the lady's forehead. Mrs. Dell didn't respond. She didn't respond to anything now. Thin, ancient, she held on past her time, didn't know she merely existed. The nursing home sent her with horn-rimmed glasses, smudged and opaque, not cleaned, or seen through, in years.

ER 5 was cool, good for a fevered patient, but Mrs. Dell had goosebumps on pale arms. So Catie brought a single blanket from the warmer to achieve just the right temperature now that the failing body couldn't manage the task. She started an IV, gave fluid and antibiotics. The ER doc decided to wait to call the admitting doctor until eight in the morning. Mrs. Dell got what she needed, and they could watch her for a few hours in the ER.

At four fifteen a.m., Mrs. Dell's breathing pattern changed to a deep and rapid cycle, so Catie checked a blood sugar level to see if she was ketotic. She lay on her side on the gurney, eyes closed, breathing. Catie looked in the chart for the DNR, to see it with her own eyes, a practice she started in nursing school when the instructors scared her with a story of confusion over status that made a student nurse break the ribs of a cancer patient who didn't want CPR. Catie skimmed the chart for family to call. The face sheet said: "Next of Kin—none." She'll die soon, Catie thought, maybe before seven a.m. No one should die alone.

Catie sat by the bed and put the side rail down so she could hold her patient's right hand in the dark, quiet room. She took the washcloth from her forehead and hung it over the rail; she would get a new one in a few minutes. It was rare to be still. Catie studied her hair, white and a bit straggly, little ringlets like a baby doll's lay sparsely on her head. Someone brushed it recently. Catie loved to have her hair brushed for hours. The lady's hands were fragile, bones prominent, skin white and tissue thin but with the warmth of fever and life, veins like blue straws over the knuckles. Her IV was easy. She breathed in and out. It was the only thing she did anymore.

Catie started a life story for her; she couldn't verbalize her own. She was kind to her children and stray cats. She dressed them in nice clothes, the children, and bathed them, even the cats. She lived in a modest house and kept it clean. She cooked wonderful meals, recipes from Italy, and her sauce found fame in the neighborhood. She never rode a horse and kept no dogs; she was allergic to their kibble. She had fashion sense and avoided bell-bottom jeans and tube tops, although she was probably fifty then, so it was an unlikely temptation. She read *Vogue* magazine and wore colors that matched and sophisticated fabrics; no fish for her.

Tina opened the door and peered into the dim room. "What are you doing?"

"Do you need me?" Catie tossed her the washcloth. "Will you wet that? The Tylenol hasn't brought her temp down yet."

"No, don't need you. What are you doing?"

She was sitting at the bedside of an unresponsive patient in a dark and quiet room. She was waiting with her. Waiting with her to die. The hours she spent wouldn't count against Mrs. Dell's remaining time.

Tina ran water over the washcloth and looked over her shoulder at them. "Catie?"

She patted Mrs. Dell's hand as Tina replaced the cloth on her forehead. Catie said softly, "We're just waiting."

Acknowledgments

Special thanks to my wonderful designer, Stacey Aaronson, who brought this to life in just the way I imagined.

About the Author

Photo credit: Linda Blue Photography

JO TAYLOR is a retired ER nurse who grew up with three stepmothers (not at the same time), has lived on a boat in Santa Barbara Harbor with her husband and her dog, and can trace her genealogy to the year 310.

A writer at heart all her life, Jo dove into the endeavors of poetry and short story writing to develop craft and style. Her first story won Honorable Mention for *Glimmer Train* in 2009, and a handful of poems and short stories have since been published in literary magazines. *Postcards* is the result of her desire to have a collection of her work in hand, if only to prove to herself that her literary labors are tangible.

Jo has been married for years and has one grown son. She is also a psychic medium, mostly in retirement from performing readings, but retains the gift nonetheless. She currently lives in Daphne, Alabama.

Connect with Jo:
jotaylorauthor.com • x.com/jotaylorauthor